# Salute the Word

# Salute the Word

## PROFESSOR M.R.ALI

Matador
9 Priory Business Park
Kibworth Beauchamp
Leicestershire LE8 0RX, UK
Tel: (+44) 116 279 2299
Fax: (+44) 116 279 2277
Email: books@troubador.co.uk
Web: www.troubador.co.uk/matador

ISBN 978 1783060 351

British Library Cataloguing in Publication Data.
A catalogue record for this book is available from the British Library.

Typeset in Aldine by Troubador Publishing Ltd

**Matador** is an imprint of Troubador Publishing Ltd

# Contents

# *Introduction*

(IAAC) The International Association of Art Critics in Sweden has inspired the writing of this poetry book.

I was asked by the Mayor of Stockholm, who gave a buffet reception at the city hall to an international delegation, to read one of my poems. I was delighted and I read the poem 'Stockholm is a darling city'. To my surprise I received rapturous applause from the audience and the recognition of the Mayor, who asked for a copy of the poem and my signature!

At the time I realised that words are more powerful than all the paintings which we had seen in art galleries and museums at the beginning of our trip. I noticed that paintings, unlike poetry, have no language barrier. Words can move people's feelings regardless of their mother tongue. Body language is another factor that enhances poetry and contrasts with a still statue at the entrance of a museum or a painting on a wall.

My visit to Sweden had encouraged me to exchange the brush and palette for words and verses. Exploring the art of writing poetry demonstrated the diversity and richness of languages and its influence on my thought process.

I still think in Arabic yet write in English, this allows me to anglicise Arabic words and inject English ideas with an Arabic perspective.

The content of this poetry book 'Salute the Word' is testimony to the power of words and ideas; a fascinating journey from one language to another and from one culture to another, leading us, ultimately to familiarity.

In conclusion, Rudyard Kipling stated that words are the most powerful drug used by mankind, how right he was.

Two of our five senses, speaking and hearing, are word orientated. Words make us happy or sad and words can make us capable of love or hatred, words can even make us learn.

About the Poet

An Anglo Arab poet with a B.Sc. degree from the University of Wales and a Ph.D. from London University is exploring a new way of writing poetry. His early career began in engineering and in teaching before he switched to art.

He believed that science and art could work in harmony. He founded the concept of 'Artology' and then 'Deltaism' as post cubism. He went on further by inventing the Deltar, a patented musical instrument derived from mathematics.

His love of poetry started in Kerbela, Iraq, his place of birth. At that time he was a keen poetry reader and studied Arabic poetry and literature. In time his interests shifted from engineering and science to poetry and literature.

The unique quality of his exploration of poetry is the combination of his scientific knowledge in English and his background in Arabic poetry, which cumulates in descriptive poems of various themes and topics in the English language.

His previous three poetry books 'Poems of the Cities', 'Poems for Art's Sake' and 'Echo of Wars' are the start of an adventurous attempt to break down the barriers between disciplines, cultures and languages.

With 'Salute the Word' the poet has shown poetry to be more global than local.

# From Culture to Culture

# *The Pen*

The pen is a faithful friend of the human being
The pen is the unknown soldier of learning
What does the pen think?
What does the pen drink?
What does the pen do for a living?

Writing is one of the pen's many careers
The pen drinks the ink of ideas
The pen is the warrior of all warriors
The pen is clever
The pen is power

From early times
The pen of wisdom
Shone on the horizon
Of every kingdom,
The pen had its place
In the forefront of the human race

The books that had been written
From fiction to religion
Has led civilisation
To future aspiration
The pen and its guidance
Through the journey of reliance

Have you heard of the Shakespearean pen?
Rattling now and then
Conceiving play after play
The famous dramas of the olden days
The pen is a writer
The pen is an actor

The pen is a rapier by its own right
The pen can fight and fight
The pen can write and write
From the left or from the right
The pen can do anything
It has more influence than a king

The pen keeps his word
The word is not afraid
To be heard or to be read
The pen has a force
And the authority of a boss

The pen is funny
The letters he writes are many
Some are romantic
And some are dramatic
The pen can be naughty
But prefers to be sporty

The pen can shout
Without any doubt
In silence he is fearful
His writings can be tearful
The pen has his mood
Which quite often, can be rude

The pen leads the way
In a dark or bright day
Sketching what may
And writing what we say
The pen is a helpline
The pen is a lifeline

In sorrow and loneliness
A pen is all you need
Let the pen be your friend
He is a friend indeed
The pen is faithful
And to you is lawful

The pen tells the truth
The pen writes the lies
The pen can make you laugh
The pen can make you cry
Homage to my pen!
That flies so high

# The Key

I am the key
I am the key
Let me be
Your trustee
Let me be
In your custody
You and me are meant to be
To open the door of opportunity

I am the key of the city
I am the key of happiness
I am the Keywest
I am the key of the rest
I am the key of open sesame
I am the key of secrecy
I am the key
Don't lose me

I am the decorated key of history
With the ability and command
To lock and unlock the genie of mystery
And to open the gates of heaven
Now I am in your hand
Don't misuse me
I hope you understand

# Deep in my Thought

In the depth of my thought
I wrote a plot
To discover a lot
Believe it or not
The plot unfolded as I thought

Tying each knot
Of an intricate plot
Needs a lot of thought

To reach the chain of thought
To make the plot workable
We need to master
The possible and impossible

To divide the roles between
The players and the plotters
Everyone has the vision to see
And to be agile and approachable
For the sake of being
Part of a cake
Doesn't matter how much it takes

Asleep or awake
The job has to be done
In secrecy

Back to the plot
The players and the plotters
We have to add the victims and the winners
So the plot is complete in one episode
Without blood or tears
Three cheers for the plot
Without a name or title
Or even substance

# The Serder

I am a Serder, I serd like a bird
A word chases another word
The diction that you heard
And the way it is read
Spins everybody's head


Now let us serd together
With a deep feeling to one other
Like a Serder serds a surrender
Let the words travel further
On doves' wings forever


The Serder is everybody's friend
Serding stories will never end
Serding is the new transcending trend
Be a Serder like me and pretend
You have discovered the right musical blend


★  Serder is an anglicised (Arabic) word derived from 'Serd'. It is used by
   badeons or town criers. To tell a story or the news of the day. Therefore 'to
   serd' is synonym 'to narrate'

Give her all you can give
And in happiness you will live,
Giving is living
And living is giving
To give is to live


Give her all your love
She gives you the sky and above
Giving is loving
And loving is giving
To give is to love

# *Endurance*

If you have a will, you endure
Perseverance, never retreating is a cure


To endure you need will power
Then by yourself you will discover


Your inner strength and resistance
To preserve your existence


With confidence and tolerance
You endure with resilience


The unexpected struggle
To put you on top of the hill


Endurance is will
And always will

# Escapade

My escapade is to escape from reality
My escapade is to seek eternity
To escape or not to escape

My escapade is a self-made illusion
To achieve comfort in seclusion
To escape or not to escape

My escapade is to find the truth
And look back at my passing youth
To escape or not to escape

My escapade is to be a tramp escapee
Just happy roaming free
To escape or not to escape

My escapade is to be a big star
Without you, I will never reach that far
To escape or not to escape
It is up to you!

# The River

Life is a river
Both are similar
They flow forever
From wherever to whenever

The river is forever
And life is an endeavour
To obtain whatever
The river is a mirror

It reflects the lovers
Of nature and greenary
Tall mountains reclining
On beautiful scenery

It all starts
From droplets of rain
Flowing vigorously
Like blood in a vein

To a new destination
Part of the cycle
Of circulation
Keeping life in fixation

The river is a treasure
Which you may discover
When swimming in its streams
Past glory, memories and dreams

Discover what has
Never been discovered
The eternal language
That tells a story

The story of the river
Its muddy and clear waters,
The mud and the flood
Brings life to others

The angler and roar of the river
The fear of the settlers
Combined together
Bring disease and fever

Wiping away all surroundings
Clearing the way
For a new settlement
To shelter a new stranger

A new life for better days
Growth in the land
With wheat, barley and hay
If we understand

The repeated stories of the river
The river is the master
Into its domain we enter
Drinking its water without a hangover

Let the river flow
With gold and silver
Life is a treasure
So is the river

# My Grandfather

I often wonder
If I got the right picture
Of my Grandfather

I often wonder
If my Grandfather
Got my right picture

Exchanging pictures of each other
We are both similar
In looks and in character

But on Saturday Night Fever
The Grandson is better
Than the old master

Now that I am a Grandfather
And I wonder
Who has done better?!

# The Barber of Exeter Street

The Barber of Exeter Street
Dancing on his feet,
To the rhythm of the comb and scissors
What music, what a beat!

With such a tune you will be welcomed
As you enter for a treat,
With a smile you will be gestured
To a seat

While waiting your turn,
You will learn
From others, the stories
Of what they earn or what they yearn.

Reading papers while you wait,
Overhearing other people's love and hate,
Indulging in the topics of the day,
In an improvised, friendly way.

You gradually start feeling
That your turn is nearing.
You are next for a hair trimming,
And next in line for gossiping.

Be prepared to say something,
To keep chatting is the rule.
Don't be quiet, just pretend,
All you hear is important.

Do agree on what he says,
Relate to him as he talks,
Then you will find,
A few more things will be learned.

Standing as a conductor,
For conversation and news.
The exchanging of opinions,
Between one another's views.

Such a chatty feeling
Is part of the setting,
Like the mirrors on the walls,
And the bright light from the ceiling.

Talk of all shades,
Soothes your nerves,
To calm you down for
The scissors and the blade.

A silent Barber is not usual
And cannot function,
Part of his work is to keep talking
From beginning to end.

Every customer has a hair style
And a favourite talking topic,
That is why a happy customer
Comes again and never changes.

Clever Barbers are advertisers
For products and events,
From contraceptives to eau de colognes,
All gossip, entertainment and what is on.

My Barber is ready with all answers,
Just ask about any subject
From diseases to stock markets
All answers are trimmed and tailored.

Now it is time to see
The purpose of such salons
Just remember, gent's hairdressers
Became famous for their services.

Some started circumcising,
Others hair styling and manicuring,
But our dear Barber,
Continued with his usual.

All newcomers are not barbers,
Hair stylists and hair designers,
Unisex for ladies and gents,
All requests can be met.

Music and coffee as you enter,
All hair styles on display,
Now the Barber looks different,
A smart actor, not a friendly talker.

Nowadays you have choices,
What to choose is not a problem,
But I remain faithful
To the blade of my old barber.

Exeter Street Salon
Was the place for students
Of my college, recommended at that time,
For its cleanliness and nearness.

The first time I entered
All I could see,
Was an active salon of three,
Serving customers all the time.

All décor was correct,
A nice shop for that purpose,
Selling this and selling that,
Hair lotions and other items.

Then I left for some time,
A long time for such a thing,
To stay intact as before,
The address still the same.

Now the three have become one,
The service is as before.
Most shelves look deserted
And most chairs need repairs.

Now the barber is becoming older
And his clients keep dwindling,
But his spirits keep marching
To the end of every day.

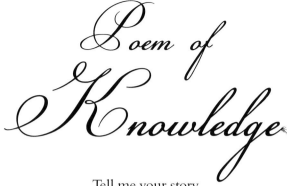

# Poem of Knowledge

Tell me your story
And I'll tell you mine

I love poetry
If you don't mind

Recite the poetry that brings memories
In physics, chemistry and geometry

Give me your time
And take my speed
(Physics)

The distance between us
Is zero indeed

Give me your gravity
And feel my spin
(Engineering)

In a vortex together
We always win

Give me your molecule
And you take mine
(Chemistry)

Your chemistry, dear
Is always fine

Show me your interests
And take my share
(Economics)

Credit or deficit
Is it always fair?

Read the stars
And feel free
(Astrology)

Tell me the story
Of Adam and Eve

Doctor of hearts
Please touch my wrist
(Medical)

The gypsy said
I should not resist

The mathematician said
He always believes

The right angle
Is ninety degrees
(Mathematics)

Circle the area
Where the pyramid lies
(Geometry)

And spot the delta
From distant skies

From low tech to high tech
And then to a higher tech
(Technology)

Does that mean
We keep on hiking tech

Science and art
Are not miles apart
(Artlology)

Believe it or not
Artlology is a start

# Noisy Lad

Noise is the sound
That goes round
Around and around
And is never bound

Noise is what you hate to hear
From far or near
Noise is fear
Oh dear!

Noise makes you mad
And it makes you sad
But it is not that bad
To hear a noisy lad

# Taste of Love

When I was a child
I was my mothers' pride
She was on my side
When I laughed or cried
That was a taste of love

I knew the truth
When I became a youth
When a lass loves a lad
Making each other mad
That is a taste of love

In the age of innocence
A touch of excellence
Love in silence
Is the love of substance,
That is a taste of love.

# City Travellers

We City Travellers do care
For our habitat everywhere
Clean water and fresh air
Yes Sir, Yes Sir
We care


We City Travellers make it pretty
Living in every city
Love, peace and eternity
Yes, it is our identity
Our city is pretty


We City Travellers grew
In every street and avenue
Accustomed to each others' views
Yes, it is true
As friends, we grew

We City Travellers work and play
Sing and dance every day
Bringing joy in every way
Our city will stay
Hey Hey


We City Travellers make it better
We travel together for our future
Holding hands the world over
We are a global band forever
Singing city songs for each other


Yes Sir, Yes Sir
We care

# Tomorrow

The present has to be
The past of tomorrow

The thought has to be
Small and slowly grows

The chaos has to be
An order and tuned into law

The love has to be
Divine, not so and so!

The life has to be
Friendship above and below

# Poema Time

I am Poema
Of rhyme and rhythm
Every day, I discover
A new 'ism'

I am Poema
Of the poetry glory
Every day, I discover
A love story

I am Poema
On the stage
Every day, I perform
Like a bird in a cage

I am Poema
Of a style
Every day, I perform
For you, with a smile

I am the poetic Poema
I hope you understand
I am the captive performer
In your hand

Do you understand?
You are my Poema!

★ Poema is a new word coined by Professor Ali, it stands for a poetic concept such as – Poema mama loves the drama!

# Second Selection

# The Cucumber Epic

I am the cucumber looking at you
I hope you do not think I am being rude
I am just in a chatty mood
I would like to tell you who is who
In the family of the cucu
I am known as cucu the true
Descendent of the cucubitaceae family
A super family that lives merrily
From China to Sicily
Filled every belly
From royalty to the willy-nilly

We look well and healthy
Dressy and wealthy
We are fresh and pricey
Salty and spicy
In the mouth we are tender
On dishes, superior
To others who so jealous
They know we are precious

See how many clans we have
And the fans we love
The cucumber is a class leader
I like to stay in the centre
With my brothers and sisters
To speak for others

On the far right is the pumpkin clan
Known as the king of Pan Pan
Brought up in Yan Yan
Grew up in Iran
And exported to Taiwan

On the near right is the melon
The delicious melon grown in Babylon
A clan with variety
Loving to mix with high society
Watermelon is juicy
And not at all saucy

Such qualities gave it trouble
Devoured by the people
Because of its size it could not travel
And its colour is visible
To avoid that
The melon had a new start
Losing weight was the answer
And a touch of new colour
Taste and odour

The young melon is now able
After the old generations gamble
To have a new timetable
With the right label
All melons became respectable
Now you see them everywhere
Displayed with style and flair
All kinds on show
Oh-ho Yo-Yo


So much for the melon
Let us go on

To my near left
Stands another clan wearing a belt
His face is like asphalt
Because he was dating the aubergine
But in fact he is more green
As can be seen
He is called the squidgy squash!
He always rushes
In a dish-dash walk
He loves dark folk
For no reason

The squash likes to be beaten
He hates to be cooked
And served as sautée
He likes to be free
With his crazy friends to be
Doing what he likes
And riding motorbikes

★ 'dish-dash' is an Arabic word for a man's nightshirt

Starting the habit
Of driving in the funny hours of the night
With high speed driving on the right
With his dodgy friends
Following behind
And what did they want to find?
A café serving Hubble bubble
Mysterious kites to fly
Fighting and laughing
Until the morning light
And then they quietly go back to hide

That is the story of the squash
With numerous crashes and splashes

See on the centre left, who is that?
The marrow is wearing a hat
We need to study it carefully
And purposefully

To see his role in high society
To which he gives priority
We know the marrow is a V.I.P fellow
Who is hollow and narrow
Like an arrow
Who has wings like a sparrow
And who likes to walk in the meadow
That is why the marrow
Gets stuffed every time
And loves the limelight
He can act and mime
Creep and climb

The marrow knows what to do
He has an independent view
Of what to cook and what to chew
His friends are the selected few
But their circle is very nice
Served with sauce and rice
Or served as nouvelle cuisine
For the has-beens
And sometimes the Queen

And to the far left
Is all that is left
The courgette
The yellow courgette is a junior member
Now he is very popular
With an attractive bright colour
Courgette is delicious
But also suspicious
Because he has a split personality

He is crisp and tender
And slightly fleshy with a moist texture
He is so versatile
You can cook him in any style
But he can be so volatile
When he loses his smile
But it takes a while
For a baby vegetable to be agile
And build its profile
In due course a few tricks
It picks
So much for the youngest member
Of the super family

Now we have completed
The order of the clans
We will talk about the fans
As I am the cucumber
Telling the story
As clan leader
Of cucubitaceae's glory
I may keep a secret or two

Let us go through
Listing what I can do
From old to new
And how I grew
To be cucu the true
I will give you a clue
When I was young and tender
I was called gherkin
And I was shaken
When they touched my skin
Nevertheless I was taken
And threatened by every chicken

That is why I preferred
To be called gherkin the pickle
So that I could tickle
The daughter of the fickle
And when I saw mother hen
Then I could giggle.
With acidity,
I gained respectability.

I slowly grew with
The neighbourhood's friends
It was the trend
To mix with the lot
But I preferred the carrot
She was musical
While I was practical
We were both ethical
Never cynical
But sometimes critical

The carrot became my childhood friend
I called her ginger
She called me sweet tender
We grew together
To be world features
Admired by our customers
And consumers
Loved by our fans
And other clans

I grew slowly from a gherkin
To a water cucumber
With shiny skin and quite slender
Loved by teenage fans
Who eat me when they can
As their superman
I felt it in my spine

I was eaten but never beaten
As the water cucumber
I was on offer
From spring to early winter
You could find me everywhere
From Kabul to Istanbul
Was always cheerful
Because I grew in the sun
And fresh air

I hate green houses
Unlike my big brother
Who doesn't bother
He grows bigger and bigger
You find him in the summer and winter
Wrapped in cellophane
To keep in his moisture
You find him in grocery shops
And supermarkets
But nevertheless
He behaves like me
As we are all from
The same family tree
We can also change colours
From green to yellow
We can be sour or hollow
We come in all sizes
And lovely varieties

Our smell, odour and perfume
Are loved in high society
We look healthy and clean
This is why everybody is so keen
It is why we are in such demand
That people can barely understand

The answer is that we
Are a unique brand
You will find us in every land
From Thailand to Switzerland
On banquets we look grand
Stylish and elegant
And quite frequently
Manicured and sculptured
To suit the occasion
Without frustration
We have a long tradition
We can suit any mixing
And any fixing
We can sing any ballad
And suit any salad

We are not self-centred
And we are good natured
We have a distinct culture
From our past to our future
And in the fields we cover
From art to sport and further
We have won prizes and awards
We have excellent records
We stand high in the crowds

As in every epic and story
The cucumber glory
Started one day in the morning
Without warning
And without asking
A new task was bestowed on me
To be Prince Charming
Of Cucumber land
Hand in hand

With my carotene darling
We set a new agenda and rules
Sponsoring healthy eating
And genetic breeding
In every meeting
We agreed
To spread the teaching
Of feeding and breeding
As Prince Cucu
And Lady Ginger
(As I call my carotene darling)
We set out together to conquer
Every menu
We wrote a list of who is who
So that everyone knew
Our view
The tomato and the pepper
Agreed with us.

Lettuce, spinach and asparagus
Wanted to discuss
The poor cabbage
Did not have the courage
Some made noises and fuss
Without success
All the menus in the land of food
Now carry our marks

After achieving
The healthy eating task
What else could we ask?
Instead we had the courage
To announce our engagement and marriage

On our wedding day
My Ginger and I were driven
In a caravan
With flowers thrown
By our followers and fans
The news was spun
Everybody got out of bed
And all heard and read
That I, the Prince Cucu
Now the figurehead
Of Food land, the wonder of Wonderland
And on my side Lady Ginger
Now we can be entered in the list of honour

As we were driven
We were given a welcome
That only seldom is seen
By a crowd that keen
With well wishers
For our next adventures
Soon after our honeymoon ended
We were requested
To continue the work we had started

With pleasure we accepted
And decided
To get the world rid
Of obesity and starvation
By intensive courses in education
We needed to start a new direction
A new book on how we look
On how we eat and cook
Carotena darling knew the answer
Start teaching the world
about healthy eating

What is better than starting
'Cucumber schools for fitness'?
To discover the goodness
And richness in ourselves`

# Sinjab from Punjab

An enterprising squirrel
Worked from sunset to sunrise
To create a global enterprise
Named Sinjab from Punjab
It had for every park
A logo of a
Squirrel pushing a silver barrel

Ads on every channel
Terrestrial and international
Were transmitted
With the message

'To world squirrels
Let's get united
Behind a squirrel dream scheme'

Soon the answer came
All squirrels gave their names
As a world wide squirrel community
With the help of a mouse

They worked as volunteers
For three years
And then as shareholders
In the Sinjab from Punjab dream scheme
Networking from dusk to dawn

Across the globe
To include the snobs
Some selected yobs
A few of the nabobs★

To the tune of the squirrels anthem
With a complimentary symphony
To go with it

The anthem chorus was
'We are here and there
And everywhere
Whenever wherever
You call us – and we deliver'

A study group was formed
To outline
The marketable line
Of the online business

★ slob

And to avoid
The mess of ambiguity
And to stick to clarity
Just mention the word
'NUT'

If you have the guts
Just the right cut
Then you'll love the nut

Back to clarity and marketability
Just mention
'Nut for you?'
That is better
We are getting closer
Peanut butter, walnut
Chestnut covered with sugar
Now, it doesn't matter
The answer is clear

'Nut for you'
Whenever, wherever
We deliver!

Sinjab from Punjab's boss
Had a clever idea in mind
Squirrels are not farmers
They are neither manufacturers
Nor end-users

But they are transporters
Couriers and store keepers
Their speed and size
Are assets to any enterprise

The boss directed the study group
To spread the scoop
That nut soup
Keeps a healthy troop

Soon the good news came
From the mayor of the London
Branch of 'Squirreldom'
In the United Kingdom
He was considering grooming
The chestnut trees
In every park in the country

The boss squirrel
Took the gamble
And jetted in as a flying squirrel
In a style that marvelled,
The first among equals,
To make a special business offer
To the London Mayor – in person

To introduce and to induce
The programme and the plan was
Devised and adapted by the study group
'Nut for you?'

The Mayor was puzzled
To see the boss squirrel
In person

He introduced him
To Her Majesty the Queen
This is Sinjab from Punjab
He is keen to clean
Every park until it shines like a spark
It can be done in the dark

Every park has a clerk
And a Pontiac or Cadillac
(The technology is from Iraq)

The Queen was delighted
With her Mayor and the offer

Soon it became known
And all understood
The boss squirrel
Had a deal in hand

After this success
Now to the business of discovery
'For what is a nut?'

Work started in earnest
To achieve the best of the best
And leave the rest
For the squirrels to invest

Once the details were known
The demand had grown
To sign up the ideal miracle deal

In no time all countries and dignitaries
From around the world signed with
Sinjab from Punjab's global enterprise

They had nothing to lose
And only to gain

The boss squirrel had the pain
Of delivering what he offered

Everyone was waiting
For the formation of 'nutworking'
And the R&D★ of the study group

In the group, there was a mouse in a house
Watching and monitoring the nutworking
And the virtual happenings

★ Research and Development

The report came
From every world port
There is a secret plot
Of some sort

It's coming from outer space
To destroy the human race
Without trace
By poisoning the nut soup
After stealing the copyright outright
From the internet
Intending to upset and destroy the asset
Without regret

The mouse sitting
In his internet nest
Saw the plotters
Well dressed
Downloading the nutworking

In no time he operated
The secret code
To give the wrong decode
Giving the plotters the disinformation

Putting them out of action
To save the project
From a direct hit

The boss squirrel was busy
Building the gigantic setting
On its environmental impact
And how people act and react
And indeed this is a fact

The project had a golden heart
Right from the start
Because of its noble aim
And its name
'The greatest project of all time'
Serving people of all races

The project was split into

Collecting the nuts
Storing,
Processing,
Transporting
And distributing

Squirrels all over the world
Started collecting nuts of all kinds
To feed mankind

The nuts were stored in purple barrels
Through specially designed funnels
The outlet was a state of the art machine

The 'Nutty Processor'

This device chipped the nuts into molecules
And then into micro capsules

The outlet was connected
To a Nylon-Teflon pipe
Only a few millimetres in diameter

The inside and outside
Were coated with oxide
And dioxide
And carbide of rare metals

To act as a pulsator, ejector
The mixer adds a cooker

As the nut molecules
Sped inside the small pipe
At the speed of light
The earth's magnetic and atmospheric pressure
Keeps the pipe floating
Around the globe
Like an invisible rope

Crossing seas, continents and oceans
To specific destinations
Where subscribers had access
A button they could press
From their address

The feeder knob
To unload the micro capsule
The new human food
In the form of expanding extrude
One capsule is enough
For each meal

It has everything
That the human body needs
It has proteins, vitamins
Carbohydrates and minerals
And above all glucose and sugar

During the high speed movement
Each micro molecule collects
Free oxygen, nitrogen
And carbon dioxide
From the outside

The air filters around and
Over land, that's all
What a simple recipe
To make ideal capsules
Filled with nut soup to feed
The world's troop of people

People start living longer
Healthier and happier,
And above all
The project has continuous capacity
To supply the world its needs
Soon the global enterprise of
'Nuts for you?'
Whenever, wherever
We deliver
Rendered McDonald's and other
Fast food restaurants useless!

They are expensive, unhealthy
And uncompetitive
So the report by the study group stated.

All squirrels around the world
Were delighted by the news
Dancing and jumping
Listening to the squirrels'
Anthem and symphony
The world is in harmony
Even royal palaces
Switched to the new diet

A year on, to celebrate
The first anniversary
All royalists of the world
Gathered in London
In the presence of
Her Majesty the Queen
To honour special subjects
And on top of the list
Was Sinjab:

'Lord
Sinjab from Punjab
The habab'★

Even the mouse was not forgotten
He became:

'The mouse
Of
Windsor House!'

★ Arabic, means 'likeable'

# Human Epic

.*'Look at me, eye to eye, you and I.*
*Read each others minds*
*If you don't mind.*
*Let us coin a phrase*
*Any action of the human race*
*And to see, eye to eye, you and I*
*If the human race has an epic*
*Let us go to the basics'*

Each epic is based on the human dynamic
Like mechanics in arithmetic
The epicentre understands
Because understanding is the essence of knowledge
If you cannot understand
Even worse, misunderstand, you become isolated
From reality
And that results in detachment.

Detachment is not necessarily
The mother of ignorance
Because ignorance has a sister called blessing
And that is
'Ignorance is a blessing'

Back to the understanding
Why should you understand something?
When you don't need to understand everything in life
You are not going to be Einstein or Hawkins
You will only understand
Full stop.
Then you hope one day, something will come your way
Then you can use your knowledge
That was in your brain, in mental storage
We will come back to that.
But for now, let us see and agree
Whatever the case may be
That you and I or me and you
Have a problem understanding
I am the writer and you are the reader.
We want to prove that we understand each other,
About everything.
Before you understand you and me
We need to understand ourselves.
That is logic!
Here the question arises
How much do you want to understand?
How much?
We will never fully understand ourselves
Human beings are illogical.

One day we are like this
One day we are like that
We keep changing
If we change and nobody likes changed people
Then it will be difficult to understand
A mercurial person is like
A variable in mathematics.

The human becomes
Known or unknown
Constant or variable
Negative or positive
And so on…

If we go on listing
We will need a million pages like this
Let us compromise and say…
We partially understand ourselves.
That is better, so together, we can
Go further to discover human understanding.

As we know, humans are races in all places
Subjected to earthquakes and human-quakes!
So we partially understand ourselves,
Or relatively understand ourselves and that will lead us
To the complexity of the relativity theory.
Naturally, we want to keep
Our understanding nice and simple.
So our knowledge is just right
And adequate for its purpose.
This means we must not overload our mental storage.

If we overload our brains with unwanted strain
You have no gain, just pain.
Just imagine that you know a hundred languages
And speak them all fluently
What would you do with such knowledge?
You will probably have no time at all to use them
You may use ten at the most.

Just imagine…
In one room there are ten people
Who can only speak one language
You are the only one who can speak ten languages
What would happen?
There would be a communication breakdown
Or if the ten people could not understand each other
And you could – so what!

If everyone says 'Clinton'
They will all understand that one word,
But no more!
Is it President Clinton?
The card company called Clintons?
Or is it the Clinton Club?

You are the only one in the group
Who would have the knowledge
To enable everybody else to understand
To which Clinton they refer.
Once you start explaining, that's when
The chaos begins.
Nobody will understand anything
Because of misunderstandings
Through lack of communication.

Here we are
The more you know
The less you know
Or when you want to understand something
Finally you give up!

That is why they say
Ignorance is bliss
It is true
If you have ten knowledgeable advisors
And consultants like a big boss
Then you are blessed with knowing a lot of things
You share mental capacities with others
But such a process must have its limitations
From group to group
Whatever the reason for this limitation.

We still, have not found the solution
To human understanding
Or in a better way we are searching for a reason and counter reason
For a perfect evaluation of any situation
You find your self-indulgence in it!
Once you find that then you are happy.
If you don't find that, what can you do?
That is the question.
You cannot go on burning the candle at both ends!
That is not the answer.

For better or for worse,
We need to discover more and more ways to understand
ourselves. Understanding is learning.
The more you learn,
The more you understand,
So we need to understand the word 'learning'.
*'The process of learning*
*Starts and ends from the cradle to the grave'*
*As* the saying goes!
And who knows?!
What we learn and what we gain.
Does learning make us better?
If not then why learn.
If yes, why doesn't everyone learn?

Perhaps learning is essential;
Essential for your well-being.
We grow to learn and learn to grow –
That is how it goes!

Here we are –
Learning is a blessing
And with learning you grow and improve others.
You may achieve anything,
But you have to start from the beginning.

You learn to walk and talk –
Self learning and taught learning
Until you pass the exam or you master the skill.
You will reach your aim and play the game.
Let it be the game of life.

When we learn to survive
Life is full of games to play.
You have to learn until you are in full control of your actions;
Every move is an art and from the start you have to be smart,
To hit the bulls-eye with a dart!

Learning is never-ending
And at the end you need to use what you have learnt,
To get around in work and leisure.
And whatever you yearn for
You can learn by heart –
All the words in the dictionary.
But what happens after you have learnt every word
And are not able to use them?
– That's equally as bad!

You need to learn to put it to good use,

If your learning is weak your knowledge is weak.
Your ability to succeed becomes less and less,
Unless you reverse the process and start a new programme,
Where your software fits the hardware!
Whether you care or not,
The Internet becomes part of the set-up!

Up and up and here we go,
The Trial and Error Formula – what is that?
Firstly, you keep trying until you learn the way
To find the right way.
What happens if you find the wrong way?
Just don't take it, fake it – until you find your way,
Keep playing the game of trial and error,
Until you find the right answer in a logical manner:
Yes or no – and soon you'll know!

Whatever the outcome,
You will come to one answer –
This theory does not limit your freedom of choice.
You can choose or reject;
In effect you can conclude,
For example, your best friend is weak and in need of some advice!
How can you give advice
If he is not listening?
His ears are closed,
So you have to impose some sort of control
None of us like control.
Who controls has no easy role.
Controlling is not about losing freedom –
It all depends on the person controlling the situation.
The person who controls may well be the loser.

Controlling is not an easy matter.
Take a sheep and a shepherd;
Take a student and a teacher;
Take a soldier and an officer.
You can conclude it is easier to be a sheep,
A student or a soldier
For the obvious reason:
Who wants to take the responsibility?
Who wants the responsibility without the authority?
And if you have both you are asking for chaos!
People reject this.
People don't understand.
People hate you for limiting their freedom
And they turn against you.
Whilst you are controlling their lives
They are in fact controlling yours
In reality, both are acting like control freaks,
For no reason, like a catch 22,
Like the egg and the chicken,
Like the enemy within.
Now you would believe that humanity is shattered!
You cannot control yourself,
Let alone control others.

This will lead us to the types of control and the art of control:
Family control, media, state, machine, nature etc.
Is it addictive to control?
Is it destructive to control?
Is it constructive to control?
Is it seen or is it unseen?
Love is one type of control
Fear is one type of control
Money is one type of control
These can all be controlling and through them you can control others!

Let us start coining and phrasing ideas,
Before we come to the conclusion
Whether there is a Human Epic and where it is.
It is simple.
Let us name the three Epics:
The Sumerian (Gilgamesh)
The Finnish (Kalavala)
And The Greek (Odyssey).

The first was a strong king who managed to control his subjects
The second was the weather (moon, sun, cold and darkness),
This controlled nature.
The third was a tragedy,
This controlled the society.

In all these Epics
The people were misused.
Humanity cannot function without
Someone or something controlling it!
The entity in control needs to use all the instruments of power,
Including all forms of knowledge,
Seen or unseen!
Humans achieve countless feats countless defeats!
But it is not yet an Epic.
Gradually a person in control
Starts to understand brotherhood and sisterhood,
This is on the path to achieving this Epic.
One day, when the Human Epic is crystallised,
It will be known as **"The People's Epic"**

'The more you know the less you know,
*Does it mean –*
*The less you know the more you know?*
*What you know*
*Is what you know*
*More or less?*
*We start knowing*
*Each other*
*To excess'*

# *Lovers around the World*

Love is virtual
Love is spiritual
Love is a ritual
Love is visual
Love is mutual, sexual and sensual
Love is physical, contractual and tactile

Love is multi-dimensional
Love is a perpetual game
Played with the aim to win acclaim

When you master the rules
Find the saints and the fools
Love becomes the game of life
And the test to survive
Which for love
Is why we all strive

You hear the baby's cries
Part of his mother's womb
Is this a sign of love?
Or living?
Like a blossom continuing to bloom
Or is this love from the beginning?
Isn't a baby's love a blessing?

Professor M.R. Ali | 77

From the womb's darkness and threshing
Love shows us the way
When life glitters with brightness
And the baby starts to play
Isn't love like this pure kindness?

The child in his mother's arms
Is a sign of love and harmony
Full of hopes and charm
And to each other, great company
That is love and its testimony

The mother and a child
Are a symbol of love and peace
They are side by side
Playing seek and hide
Love is a maternal stride
The young grow older
We all need each other
Diversity in love
Becomes the order
And takes over
Youth likes to differ
Nobody has the answer

Youth has its love story
How many times the young feel sorry
Because they missed the last dance
And maybe something happened to the romance
Remember, love starts with a glance

Take an epic journey in love's land
You firstly, need to understand
Love has no command
Secondly, love is a demand
Yes, love is a demand

Let your tour start
Wrap your feelings in love's art
A part of a bigger part
Does love tick in your mind or heart?
Yes, love is surely from the heart

Let love be our guide
In this wonderful ride
And what we find
Is that love is truly blind
Yes, love is truly blind

Never mind
Love can speak
In Greek, Chinese and double Dutch
Love softly peaks
With a velvet touch
Yes, love is a double catch

Travelling through love's venues
Its boulevards and avenues
Every lover has a view
On what to choose of love's menu
Its tasty pursuits

Love without warning
Disappears in the early morning
We are left without cover
We will cry forever
Yes, love can be pure torture

Although our trip may be ending
Our memory is fading
Our guide deserting us
Betrayed lovers without fuss
Yes, we can claim to have taken the wrong bus

Continue the search without a pause
For dear Mr Right and not Mr False
We have been cheated before
No more, no more, no more!
Does Mr Right knock on the door?

We can wait, wait and wait
Mr Right is not too late
To get it right is great
In this game of love and hate
Remember Romeo and Juliet.

Josephine loved Napoleon
Anthony loved Cleopatra
Dodi loved Diana
And ET Cetera loves ET Cetera
What about crazy Electra?!

Love is a desire
Lust and passion
It follows no norm or fashion
Love is a self creation
A triumph of the imagination
Or is love born out of starvation?

Love is a head spinner
For worshippers and sinners
When it comes, it strikes
Like the lightening before the thunder
Or does love only come in shades and colours?

Love is a sweet torment
It is a gentle controller
It fixes broken hearts
And it breaks the wise gladiator.
All the same, love needs no teacher

Now let us start again
On the lovers' fast lane
Forget all past torment and pain
We have nothing to lose and much to gain
Lovers must keep trying again and again

Yes, love is sophistication
We need the right team
To reach our destination
With a love map and theme
Yes, the right team is a dream
Of heavenly fascination

Our team is made of seven
One from each tavern of life
A lover for each season
A lover for every reason
Love is a self creation

We are the seven types of lovers
Travelling together to world wonders
Sight after sight
Flight after flight
Just to have a glimpse of Mr Right
Let him be yellow, black or white

The ultimate aim for each lover
Is finding his or her opposite number
Exchanging the secret word of feeling
So body language can start working
Love is shy and needs introducing

The King of Spain is our first patron
In his palace, partying 'til dawn
Champagne, caviar and chit chat
With open hearts, we had a good start
But in the early morning the lovers had to part

The lady of Spain bid us farewell
We part two at a time
Like a story from a fairytale
A paradigm in a lover's chime
The sublime meeting of a lifetime

On the way to our next stop
The love expedition is full of hope
From safari to Kilimanjaro's top
We see its snow covered top
From afar and love can be a slippery slope

The next romantic scene
Is set up by the African Queen
Dancing and leading pageantry
An ideal process in pleasantry
African love is pure chemistry

Arabian love and romance
Are welcome for a golden chance
With the one thousand and one nights
Lovers may meet Mr Right
As a horseman rides in twilight

The passage to India
Becomes our lovers' euphoria
They have no idea
The custom is mother superior
Each lover needs a warrior

China and Japan are kindlers
In love affairs they are wonders
Lovers are lost and found
Selling, buying and shopping around
Each love has its own particular sound

Love affairs across the Pacific
Love in Hollywood is terrific
In the supermarket of love, you pick
And on the line you get the kick
But Hollywood always has its magic

In New York, you see it all
Money and power are the goal
Rumours, scandals and jokes
Everything sunny for some folkes
Although the dollar talks and bullshit walks

Poor love is an unfinished symphony
It is funny to realise love is money
If you are rich, I am your honey
If you are poor, I leave this journey
Unfinished love always needs money

We are back where we started
But much wiser then before we parted
Around the world we have discovered
That all lovers have repeatedly suffered and
Love still needs to be uncovered

Love is elusive and intrusive
Love is private and exclusive
Public love becomes seductive
Love is everywhere but reclusive
Love is often inconclusive

Love is an empty nothingness
Unless filled with something else
Envy, sadness or happiness
To create togetherness and completeness
Love is a zero vortex of success

Love has its philosophy
Aphrodite is one of its trophies
But love remains a loving word
That is exchanged in a lover's world
Like a whispering lovebird

Lovers need a universal kingdom
A love constitution for all
With passports of adoration
A language for spirit and soul

With an earthly love currency
The outer space and its galaxy
Will welcome the next expedition
Armed with a love ray as ammunition
Martians surrender without condition
Inter-planetary love and adulation
From the first galactic station
A stadium in outer space
A lover's concert in place
Dancing together in a heavenly chase

Thank you for the company
On this epic journey
I hope you enjoyed the tour
Please, don't forget your love brochure
As you leave through the door

For now your turn is coming
For a friendly questioning
Is love everything?!
We are all ears and listening

# Roman Rhapsody

**A**  Deltacy (Roman Village)

**B**  Deltarium (Roman Rendezvous)

**C**  Deltaman (Caesar)

# Deltacy

Once upon a time
The Romans settled on the hill of deltacy
The hill with the legacy
As we will see
Let us see

On our road to a deltacy village
Where the Romans were known for their courage
We find the delta tunnel to deltacy
Carved in the trees
Carved in the trees
Carved in the trees

In a delta shape
What a beautiful landscape

In threes, in threes
We slowly move through the trees
With ease
With ease
With ease

Flowers everywhere
At the touch of a finger tip
Now we start the trip

To the land of deltacy
Through the delta tunnel of fantasy

Now you have entered a world yet to be discovered

In the deltacy world of reality
Soon you will be invited
To the Roman deltarium
To celebrate the millennium
Be ready
Be ready
Be ready

# Deltarium

Welcome, welcome
To the deltarium of dreams
Where your leisure and pleasure
Are fantasies forever

Through the rainbow
We all go
Three in a row
To your fellow, say hello
To your fellow, say hello

And soon you reach the hill
Where you feel the delta thrill

The missions begin
In deltarium heaven

With songs of the day
Dance and sway
Celebrating in the delta way

In the centre of your dream
You shout and scream
'Deltarium is a dream!'
'Deltarium is a dream!'

Touch the air
And touch the breeze
Touch my hand and whisper clear
Everybody's coming near
Everybody's coming near
To the delta gate of heaven
Where our missions will fly
On a lucky cloud seven

With the Roman Caesar
He has the answer
He is coming nearer
He is coming nearer
He is coming nearer

# Deltaman

I am what I am
I am the Roman deltaman
I am the head of the deltacy clan
I am the Caesar superman
Delto fellow Caesar
Delto fellow Caesar
Delto fellow Caesar

Fellow Romans, deltaists and others
Let your motto be…
'Deltaism holds the key!'
Let it be
Let it be
Let it be

Fellow Romans, deltaists and others…
Do you want me to be your Caesar of the century?
Yes, we agree
Yes, we agree
Yes, you will be
Yes, you will be

Let the delta we left behind
Guide us to a glorious future
Of deltacy and deltarium
Delto fellow Caesar
Delto fellow Caesar

And now, let us all pray for this glorious day
To the tune of the Deltar
One for two… and two for three
Deltaism holds the key
Deltaism holds the key
Three for two… and two for one
Deltaism is fantastic fun
Deltaism is super fun

# The Five Senses in Haiku

Haiku is Japanese poetry
Putting consonants and vowels together
In a particular manner.

With three lines
And syllables to measure
In five, seven and five.

All you can derive
Haiku is beauty
Without rhyming but full of life

That is why my five senses
Sensed another way
Equal and beauty and has tutti-fruity

That is fine
My haiku had also three lines
With a touch of a lovely cutie

# Touch

The art of touching
Is a sensual expression
Of one's feelings

That is why
Touching is accepting
And touching is rejecting

Touching conveys meaning
As in shades of colours
Smells and odours

Touching is a daily happening
Touching here, touching there
And touching everywhere

Touch and taste
Without haste
Is what lovers crave

Touch and touch
Catch and touch
And keep in touch

Touch of class
Touch of culture
And touch of fever

Touch the earth
Touch the sky
And touch me, why?

Touch me tender
Touch me please
A touch of ease

Touch me with your touch
Touch me as such
And touch me just as much

Touch my laughter
Touch my anger
But touch me eagerly

Now let us finish touching
With an un-touchy mood
Touch-wood

# *Listen*

Listen to the storm and the thunder
Listen to the crying and the laughter
Listen to the song and the whisper

Listen to the teacher and the speaker
Listen to the friend and the neighbour
Listen to the animals and nature

Do you listen to yourself?
When you need confidence
Or do you share other's guidance?

So you accept listening
To other peoples instructions
Team listening is an attraction

Listen to me
And I will listen to you
Let us see each other's points of view

Listen to the older
Listen to the younger
But never say never

Listen to your friends complain
Listen to them again and again
And learn what you can

Listen to your doctor's advice
Listen to him once or twice
Exercise self-sacrifice

Listening and learning
Living and listening
And we all need educating

Listening makes you wiser
Listening is much better
Than speaking for ever

We hear and listen
To whatever is given
As a point of discussion

But being a silent mole
Without spirit or soul
Is not bad at all

# *See*

Seeing is believing
Or is it deceiving?
Or can it be misleading?

Seeing through a crystal ball
Looking into a dark hole
A forecast of rise and fall

Seeing the right and the wrong
Seeing the weak and the strong
To see to whom you belong

Have you seen the atom splitting?
Have you seen our earth spinning?
Have you seen the moon eclipsing?

The vanishing point of sight
The focusing beam of light
The vision between black and white

Although the blind man cannot see
He has the insight to see
What we cannot see

The vision of the blind
Is seeing of a kind
Which contributes to mankind

Do you see the unseen?
Or do you like to be seen?
On the scene to be foreseen

I can see you now
Or I can see you later
Or I can see you never

I can see you far
I can see you nearer
Or I can see you closer

See with your eyes
Visualise with your mind
Look to what you find

See the candle light
Admire the lovely sight
Is it brilliant or bright?

See an action
See destruction
See an attraction

See the good
See the bad
See Mum and Dad

See the end
Watch the trend
Are you still my friend?

# *Smell*

Smell of freshness
Smell of goodness
Smell of richness

Smell the perfume
Of the bride and groom
On their honeymoon

Get close
Smell the scent of the rose
With your nose

Well well, smell
The wine, when you dine
Does it taste fine?

Sniff and sneeze
Feel at ease
Smell me please

We smell together
We smell the flower
Our love is forever

Mother's smell
On her child
As her joy and pride

What you smell
Tells your tale
Smell sweet as a treat

# Talk

Talk is a sound
Produced through the mouth
That goes round and round

Talk is a weird signal
From speaker to listener
As in a lover's whisper

Sweet talk
Roll and rock
Around the clock

Cheek to cheek
Don't play the freak
Hide and seek

Don't be murky
Talk turkey
And be funky

You heard it folks
Talk about talk
As in the moonwalk

Knock, knock
Cross talk
Who does the talk?

Let us have a joke
Money talks
And the cat-walks!

That's all folks!

# The Artist's World

## PART I

Does the colour vibrate
Or does it pulsate, to create the images
That speak languages
Of the human race?

Does time accelerate
Or does it stagnate?
How wonderful to reach and touch
The switch of time

Images of colours and compositions
Relating to expositions
That rotate around
A centre of fixation

To give a complete picture
Of what is happening
To the Artology
At its centre

Deep in the centre of fixation
Lies the centre of dreams
Where artists keep on looking
And scream

Wishing it did not exist
This mystery persists
But now and then
One cannot resist

The mystery of persistence
Gives total resistance
To those who have lost faith
In its existence

Do the colours exist?
Or do they transmit
Phantoms of imagination
Creating excitation?

Do colours reflect the mood?
If one only understood
The mixture of feelings

The cocktail of colours
Has its secrets
For the drinker
With racing thirst

Thirsty for colours
Please be kind
Reflect the images
That can blind

Do the blind see our colours?
Do we see theirs?
Or are we all colour blind?

Child of nature
Do not oppose
The waves of colour
And shimmering form

Which only respond
To the heart of fixation
And never melt
Into stagnation

Whatever you choose
You must remember
The secret colour
You

## PART II

Do you see the waves move
While the earth is spinning?
Reaching far away
To the low innings

Winning the race
In a far off place
Holding hope for us
Those who are staying

Cycle of hope
Please talk to me
Give me your attention
Tell me how to be free

Free to sketch
Free to see
Free to paint
And free to be

On a raft
Like the others
Dreaming of hope
And free to move

Move eastwards
Move westwards
Towards a dream island
Where I can rest

With my easel before me
The world behind
A more beautiful goal
No one could find

Now is the time
To go where I belong
Catching inspiration
The prize has been won

Snatches of visions
These I have hunted
Dearest occasions
To bring back home

# PART III

When the artist's eyes
Start seeking
To arrest
The right moment

Like a hunter
Who is listening
For the prey
He is waiting

Or an eagle
From above
Looks below
To his love

Or a captain
In stormy weather
Looking forward
To the harbour

Then, the artist's eyes
Find the answer

When the artist's eyes
Start seeking
For the centre
Of attraction

Like a soldier
Searching
For the target
Of destruction

Or a scientist
Searching
Deep into
An equation

Or an actor
On a stage
Working hard
For adulation

Then the artist's eyes
Find the answer

When the artist's eyes
Start seeking
To create visions with
The truthful meaning

Like a child
For a mother
What a moment
To remember

Or the brides
At their weddings
People glancing
At their dresses

In the open
Where the objects
Shine freely
To be subjects

Then the artist's eyes
Find the answer

When the artist's eyes
Start mixing
All the colours
All the forms

Now's the moment
To remember
Is it blue?
Or is it amber?

To be added
To be brighter
For the form
Means neither

When the scene needs a green
And the flower craves a yellow
Then the cottage needs a shade
And the tree bags a shadow

Then the artist's eyes
Find the answer

When the artist's eyes
Start seeing
A Picasso
Or a Dali

Then the names
Begin to ring
From the signs
Of early times

From Leonardo
To a Rothko
Art must wonder
What to wonder

From the renaissance
To the future
Crossing barriers
All the time

Then the artist's eyes
Start searching
For an aim
To his vision

Aiming first
For an art
An act of creation
Not destruction

Then the twist
Captures attention
To use destruction
Not attraction

Not so often
Such a vision
Gives an order
To disorder
Then the artist's eyes
Seek the task

When the artist's mind
Starts searching
For a name
For his art

Then the concepts
Begin falling
Into line
Catwalk fashion

Call it Pop, call it Dada
But there is
Only one answer
Learn from this
And remember

From the Delta
Came the art
From the art
You reach the heart

At last, the artist's mind
Found the answer

# Hospital

I know you well
The birth of my mother's dream
You came my way
And how can I forget you?
You do care
For whoever is in need of caring

You know me so well
Since I was born
You used to call my name
You do care
For whoever is in need of caring

You knew I would come back
Because I needed you
I had no time to ask
As I did not know what to do
You do care
For whoever is in need of caring

All the nights we spent together
As if we were meant for each other
Unaware of the real danger
Tomorrow was another day to remember
You do care
For whoever is in need of caring

I didn't know what the matter was
Young at seven I did not remember
That I needed serious medication
For some unseen reason
You do care
For whoever is in need of caring

I was kept unaware
Of what could have happened
As I was prepared
For the final inspection
You do care
For whoever is in need of caring

Next to my bed was the temperature chart
Sisters and doctors would look at it and chat
Final preparations went on behind the scenes
Discussing the outcome if they didn't succeed
You do care
For whoever is in need of caring

The final discussion came
I should wait no longer
Tomorrow is the day
For worse or better
You do care
For whoever is in need of caring

Other patients in the room
Were kept away
And that night was the night
That tomorrow may never come
You do care
For whoever is in need of caring

Everybody was alert
But I didn't know why
The impact of the happening
Made the time keep running
You do care
For whoever is in need of caring

Early morning I was cheered
With a few tablets on a plate
Slowly I felt dizzy
And all of a sudden I could remember
You do care
For whoever is in need of caring

Slowly I was taken away
And everybody else had to stay
Waiting for the news
Whether bad or good
You do care
For whoever is in need of caring

The news had arrived
The operation had gone right
The patient had survived
The danger had subsided
You do care
For whoever is in need of caring

Taken back to my room on a stretcher
Where I had to be looked after
Under the eyes of a nurse and a sister
Until the time of consciousness
You do care
For whoever is in need of caring

The gesture of a well wisher
Was the signal
For me to be happy
And take the road to recovery
You do care
For whoever is in need of caring

All were glad
When I was discharged
Back to normal
With the usual schedule
You do care
For whoever is in need of caring